Men

In

Armor

Copyright Page

Men in Armor

Self published by arrangement with the author, by Lulu Technology Co.

Cover illustration by Lulu

Cover design by Elizabeth Ludlam and Lulu

Interior text design by Elizabeth Ludlam

Lulu Technology Co.

Table of Contents

Acknowledgements

I would like to thank each and every person who has come into my life over the last few years and enriched my time on this earth beyond measure. I want to call out everyone's name but I am afraid that I might inadvertently omit a name and that just would not be right. However, I know that you know who you are. So let me say, thank you so very much. I am forever grateful for your love and support.

This book would never have come to fruition without the help of two of my dearest friends; Janet and Nancy. I want to thank you from the bottom of my heart for the many hours spent reviewing, providing feedback, and most importantly encouraging me to publish. I appreciate your honesty in providing feedback both positive and in your suggestions. I know it is not always easy to critique someone's work and you did it with integrity and compassion.

I would also like to thank my beautiful little Chelsea for donating two of her prized photographs for this book. Chelsea, you are an artist by every measure with the compassion and wisdom of someone far beyond your years. It is such an honor to have you in my life.

And lastly, I would like to thank the man who inspired me to live again, to believe in myself, to be brave and tell my story. You are an amazing human being and a delight to have in my life. Thank you.

Dedication

I would like to dedicate this book to the three men who have had a profound impact on my life; my father, my husband, and my very special friend. Each one so very different yet they are so very much alike. They share beliefs in living life to its fullest, living life with integrity, and loving with passion.

Three Wise Men

There once was a girl from way up north
She met three wise men who changed her course
They came to her from different paths
And profoundly changed her fate was cast

The first man gave her life's first breath
Taught her love, hope, integrity to his death
Always there, never alone
She learned to have a voice to sing her song
Then in a horrific flash he was forever gone

One day a stranger called her name
She turned to look – would never be the same
Charming, happy, lived life with ease
Taught her insane love and how to please
She learned true love comes with no conditions
And it is harder to stay than to walk away
One day this beautiful man fell to his knees
She fights for his life with ferocious tenacity

This girl became lost in life's low of lows
Then one lonely evening her eyes fell upon
A beautiful man who forced her to feel
His heart forever young but barricaded with steel
She received his gifts resonating through her soul
He taught her to live and feel – never give up or fold
She will fight to the end for this beautiful wise man
Self destruction not an option, she will teach him the plan

Beautiful, beautiful wise men
Molded and shaped her heart
Beautiful, beautiful wise men
So different yet not far apart

Introduction

When we think about it, I guess we all have a story to tell. This is my story. I think like most people I have had some amazing, wonderful experiences in my life as well as some gut wrenching times that I did not think I would survive. This story is about the armor we all use to survive, whether to protect ourselves while doing battle with life or using it to hide from our insecurities. It is also a story of survival and learning to be happy in the midst of chaos and heartache. It is one thing to survive life's trials and tribulations, however, it is quite another to thrive.

I truly feel blessed that my life has been so full and rich. I never could have imagined that my life would take such extraordinary twists and turns. I never imagined that a person could love so deeply, laugh so hard, hurt so much, and learn infinitum. When we give ourselves permission to experience life it is a gift like none other. Sometimes we need other people to help us with that permission. Sometimes we need to help others.

I have chosen to use commentary, poems, and illustrations. The commentaries focus on three key people and some of their amazing highs and devastating lows over the last few years. The poems on these pages are stories about real life. They are not verses to ponder the questions of the universe or to make declarations of wisdom. I am probably the last person qualified to do that. The pictures and illustrations were added to further express my feelings and thoughts.

I decided to share my experiences in the hope that others will know that they are not alone. I think that I have made every mistake on this earth that a human could make and have not led my life as most would define as normal. It has made for some extraordinary experiences and some very difficult times. But I do not think I would change a thing.

I hope my words may bring comfort, hope, and strength to those with similar stories. We cannot control how we feel, only our actions.

Enjoy.

Damsel in Distress

I am short, round, middle aged and a very pragmatic female. I have always felt that people do not consider me pretty, special, or interesting enough. I sometimes wonder if other people have the same self image. I have spent a lifetime hiding myself from the world. When I was younger I used elixirs and poisons to hide. But as my career took shape, I became more serious and practical and switched to food. I was able to insulate myself with a very safe and secure wall. I think I was so fearful of being ridiculed for my looks, my actions, and my feelings that I learned to present myself as a rock; cold, hard, unbreakable. I was so clever that I was even able to hide everything from myself. I was in a comatose state for many years and it felt like a very safe place to be. It was also a very lonely and sad place. I have always had extreme confidence in my professional life and little confidence in my personal life. I have come to realize that it is a much easier task to build barriers than tear them down. I had no idea that I had so much emotion bottled up inside of me until it started leaking out on paper. Soon the leak turned into a fire hose at full throttle.

I am the youngest of three girls. My parents worked hard and provided for us well, but were definitely focused on 'why should you' versus 'why not'. I always thought, even at a young age, that it must have been the way they were raised. It was clear, in their eyes, that I was not good enough for many things. But I was born with a tenacity and passion that would not be squelched. It annoyed my Mom to no end. Both my parents loved me and were really wonderful people. I always have and always will love them very much and have never had any negative thoughts or hard feelings toward them. They both did the very best that they knew how to do. This was my world and I made my way in the context of my surroundings. It made me a very strong, determined person. It also made me have very low self-esteem. Such is life. I blame myself for not having fixed that problem sooner. I am working on it now and can see that there are significant renovations required. I am making progress and no longer hide behind the walls that I once had constructed. The renovations will continue.

I met the warrior when I was very young and wild. I am not sure where I would be if we had not met. He helped me believe in myself regarding my career and has always been very supportive. When he fell ill, my life spiraled into a non-stop tailspin. I was heading up two large full time projects at work while I was desperately searching for doctors to save his life. I was constantly running between the east coast and west coast and from the south to the north. I felt like I was under siege seven by twenty four. There was also an abundance of family and friends who thought that I should be by his side constantly and assumed that I did not care enough. The truth is that I was under constant fear that I would lose my job and the health insurance needed to keep him alive. In the spring of 2005, my worst nightmare came true; I was laid off the day after I brought him home from a rehabilitation center. I was able to find independent consulting work but it took me away from home every week. I kept gaining weight, worked 70-80 hours a week and was under so much stress, it is a miracle that I did not drop dead from a heart attack. I was taking care of everything and everyone but me. So is it just a random coincidence that this amazing white knight should walk into my life in the middle of this chaos? He helped me want to be alive again. I started writing my stories, I made new friends, lost 70 pounds (more to go), started regular exercise, changed my appearance drastically, and was determined to overcome my fear and go to my first rock and roll concert. I love music and it somehow got dropped along with many other pleasures. I learned how to be a happy person in the middle of all the sadness, trauma, and chaos. I learned to be more honest with myself about my feelings and what I could control and not control. He helped me believe in myself on a personal level.

I don't consider myself a writer. If someone writes are they a writer? If someone strums the guitar are they a musician? Perhaps it is just a matter of perspective. I started on this journey of writing about three years ago. Words just started pouring out on paper. Writing turned out to be a sanctuary for me and the cheapest therapy a person could ask for. I have never been really interested in poetry so when my stories started taking the form of poems I questioned my own sanity. But time and a lot of encouragement from a few understanding friends have helped me reconcile and enjoy writing poetry.

For a very long time I told no one what I was doing. Eventually I did tell one person and got the courage to post a poem on my favorite website. People were very positive and supportive but I thought everyone was just being polite and had little confidence in my work until I showed some poems to a very dear friend. It was on a rare girl's weekend to New York. I was really nervous. She read my journal on the train into the city. Some of the poems made her cry. That was the very first time that it occurred to me that other people might relate to my words.

To know me is to know that I am a female warrior but like every other human being, I sometimes get distressed and need someone to hold and comfort me. I guess the bottom line is that most of the time I am strong, independent, and self sufficient. But there are days when I just need to be allowed to be the Damsel in Distress.

Hope and Fear

This darkness is soothing in a sinister sort of way
It wraps itself around me cleverly hiding the light of day
Wallowing in my sorrow rooted in my deepest, darkest fears
A sorry kind of comfort that strips life from here to there

Why am I languishing in this lonely, miserable place?
Allowing it to quietly steal every ounce of my faith
This is so unlike me to have opened this dark, dark door
And step into this dungeon of despair and hellish horror

My will is made of granite, although sometimes I wish not
The rock for all to lean on, someone hold me, I feel forgot
I must emerge from this dead, evil place
I must face tomorrow with dignity and grace

Where is my beautiful white knight?
I need a tiny glimpse of your amazing white light
Hold out that powerful, beautiful, gentle hand
Tell me I am worth just a second in your eyes

I know I can make it on my own
But just once I wish for a small reprieve
Dear knight please send me a sweet, perfect smile
And make me laugh for just a short while

I choose hope; I choose to be set free
And I pray each day that hope chooses me

My Warrior

I met him in the lounge of a Chinese restaurant when I was very young, divorced, with two toddlers. I still do not know why he didn't run as fast as he could. At the time, he was a very broken man. He had married his true love and she broke his heart. She actually shattered it into a million pieces. Neither of us was interested in getting into a long term relationship. But we were pulled together like two high powered magnets, never to part. On our first date he took me to an open house at a funeral home. It was the wildest party that I ever went to. I am told that I had a very good time.

Our life was anything but calm and normal. We played hard, worked hard, and lived in the moment. We threw parties that are now legendary and he was definitely the life of the party. Everyone loved him and wanted to be near him. Women were drawn to him like bees to honey. He was loyal and true, so I just watched with amusement. We have six children between us. He has four boys. I have the girls. The Brady bunch. We decided not to make any more babies. In retrospect, that was probably a very wise decision.

My warrior was anything but that for most of our time together. He was happy, easy going, not very driven, loved to party, and hated to fight. We were opposites. I was intense, serious, tenacious, and ready to do battle with any guilty party. I have learned that sometimes it is best when partners are alike, and sometimes it is better when they are opposites. For us, the contrasts helped balance each other out and provided for some pretty interesting times. I was insanely in love with this man. I loved him in every way one human being could love another. I loved him in every way that a woman loves a man. Insanely, intensely, unconditionally. No matter how many times I thought I was at the end of my rope, I had no option but to be with him. I loved him too much for anything else. My warrior was not always there for me in the ways that I needed. But he always loved me and always supported me. I followed my dreams which took me around the world and away from him a good portion of the time. I sometimes wonder how many minutes of his life were spent just waiting for me. He never once complained.

He encouraged and pushed me to go back and finish college. He made me feel like I could accomplish anything and trusted my judgment without question. He made me laugh when I didn't want to and held me tight when I needed it although often needed big clues.

He was the happy, strong, healthy guy. I was the serious, intense, over weight gal who smoked. It was so unfair that he was the one who got sick. Cancer attacked him with a vengeance. He fought back. The treatments caused him to have a massive stroke. He fought back. The cancer continued to attack. He turned out to be the bravest man I ever met. I speak of him in the past tense because the stroke stole his mind, personality and much of his physical abilities. The man in the Chinese restaurant is gone forever. But, as of this moment, I have the joy of waking up beside my warrior, sharing rare moments with him, and holding him tight when he needs it. People tell me how lucky he is to have me to support him. I think I am the lucky one.

I think I will probably spend the rest of my days writing about him. I have yet to find the words to truly express how much I love this man. I sometimes wonder if the words exist.

The Warrior

He dresses in silence preparing the day
Slowly facing the man in the mirror
Searching for courage there is no delay
Not his choice this battle of horror

The mighty warrior so fearless and strong
Now a shadow, but relentless in pursuit
Hidden enemy here does not belong
Attacks keep coming and now take root

I will stand with you to fight this battle
You will never, ever be alone
My strength is yours for the taking
Hand in hand we will see tomorrow

Evil lurks in dark places and strikes without warning
You think he's beaten and long since vanished
Past battle scars run long and deep
The warrior fiercely fights for victory to keep

Remember stellar days of our past
When happy was the charge of the day
A kiss, a touch felt forever to last
I pray we will see those moments again

I will stand with you to fight this battle
You will never ever be alone
My strength is yours for the taking
Hand in hand we will see tomorrow

My White Knight

I always thought that it was just a fantasy. White knights were for fairy tales and for princesses, but definitely not for someone like me. I was wrong, so very, very wrong.

The first time I saw my White Knight I was drowning in extreme, unbearable stress and turmoil. My warrior was in constant battle for his life, work was a double load on different coasts, and everyone had an opinion about what I was doing wrong and felt it their duty to tell me and tell me often. I will forever believe that he came to my rescue just in time. This story would have had a much different ending if it were not for him. I saw him from a distance. At the time, he could not see me, had no idea that I existed. If someone had told me then he would become my White Knight, I would have rolled my eyes and given my most polite yet dismissive laugh. But he demanded my attention, stole my heart, and from that very first encounter he would be in my life forever and change it so profoundly that even I became a believer.

My White Knight is intelligent, funny, powerful, gentle, controlling, intense, and a hopeless romantic. He is such a good and beautiful man on the inside. I have never met anyone like him. He is the man of every woman's dream however the man few women have the strength and knowledge to love and support. He is extremely complicated and a most intriguing study in contrasts. He can be so powerful yet so gentle, so intense yet seem so carefree, so intelligent yet misses some basic life concepts. He is the most guarded human being I have ever met, yet his life and heart are on display for anyone paying attention. He is so sensitive and yet most people do not see it. I love his forever young, tender heart and his beautiful ancient soul. When I am in his presence he is overpowering and bigger than life. However in private, I imagine he is much like the rest of us and struggles with confidence, direction, and just wanting to love and be loved. When he wraps his arms around me it takes my breath away because he is so genuine.

He showed me how to be brave about my personal life and tell my story. He made me want to live and dream again. We became friends. I don't think either of us set out for that to happen but a connection was made and it is strong and permanent. I have so many feelings towards this man and have struggled to understand them. I finally decided to stop trying to make sense of it and just delight in the fact that a White Knight showed up at my door. I can never go back to who I was before I met him.

He is my White Knight today, tomorrow, and forever.

Thank You

Hey you, my silly …
Did I ever thank you?
For the joy you have infused into my life
Your young heart and ancient soul melted my protective ice

Did I ever tell you?
I feel so privileged to call you my friend
A forever bond cast, never to be undone

It seemed almost instantly you made me believe
In myself, in tomorrow, and that again I could be happy
Refueling my desire to indulge in the pleasures of discovery

You trusted me with your emotions
Forever locked safely in my heart
You and I so unlikely from the very start

Remember that very first night?
I was rendered speechless from your warm affection
And your genuine happiness – such a divine perfection

So my beautiful, silly little friend
Whether you are here or far, far away
I promise to always hold you close forever and a day

I cherish you, always will
So just in case I forgot – Thank You

The Awakening

The year was 2006. After many years of wallowing in my self induced coma, I woke up. I felt alive, had clarity, passion, and became determined to shed the heavy armor I had so carefully created. I was excited about life again and wanted to discover new things. This was also the year that I started writing. It began slowly but gained momentum as the year progressed. It was the year that I began listening to music during my free time. Writing and music were better than any drug a doctor could prescribe.

During this year of awakening something wonderful happened. I began to feel happy. And something else happened. Everyone around me was happier too. It was infectious. Life was getting interesting.

It took something miraculous, amazing, and beautiful. It took a white knight.

Not Looking

He's in meltdown with obsession, not love
Beautiful soul, endless body, tortured mind
Simple act of kindness and her soul feels fine
One touch, just one – their fate is sealed
Female strength he never knew
Would stay the night to see him through

Recovery's quick and he's on the prowl
It's his way, he has no clue
The lady needs more, it's in her brain
Truth, trust, respect are all her game
Sex, drugs, fun is all he ever knew
Beautiful soul, endless body, she cannot refrain

She needs her life – he needs his dream
He goes on west, she heads on east
Separation makes together so sweet
They resist, but are converging forever
Love is slow, simmer to boil forever and ever

Not looking, not needing
Not wanting, not doing
One kiss, one touch, his eyes on her
Didn't want it but he has done her in
I swear to God I could never leave
Too late, you made a difference, you must believe

Where Are You?

You were my lover, my partner, my best friend
Our life – what a scary roller coaster ride
Good times, bad times, here to the end
We loved hard, cried hard, held each other when
You lived for the moment happy and true

Life plays its dirty little tricks – so I see
When you play by the books it's so unfair
How could God take you but leave you there
Here one moment, then vanished to air
I don't understand but will forever take care

Where are you I can see you, you're right there
Where are you I can't find you, you're in the chair
You're a stranger, who are you? I need you, please come back
Where are you? My lover, no longer aware

This is our future together but not
Will love you forever 'til the end
But I do need some comfort I'm the one forgot
I miss you so much it must be a crime
Need to take you back, again be mine

Where are you? I can see you, you're right there
Where are you? I can't find you, you're in the chair
You're a stranger, who are you?
I need you, please come back
Where are you?
My lover, no longer aware

It's in Her Brain

Mission impossible, over and out
My girl says she wants me
Then no, no, no
How's a man to figure it out
Touch me, then don't – confusing as hell
Please give me a handbook and please do tell

Doctor, oh doctor please help me here
Need some lov'n but my girls unclear
Doc looked me in the eye and held my gaze
Said, son, you've entered the female haze
It's in her brain
Do you hear me, it's it her brain
Don't run to the end zone
Please do refrain
Kiss her, hold her
Give her what she needs
She'll take you to the end zone
And the dirty deed

Doesn't sound right, can't be true, I said
But took my handbook to give it a try
My girl is so sexy I can't wait
I kiss her and kiss her and kiss her some more
I hold her, say I love you
We hit the floor

The ice is melting and she starts to fly

She moves closer

Her warmth is so near

She touches me

I feel so high

She guides me and directs me

Places so dear

Who is this woman? She has no fear

In heaven within her

With no way out

She guides and directs me

It can't be true

Can't believe it's so easy - Who knew?

Mission impossible, over and out

Ugly

Hide in the closet, hide in the wall
I am so ugly I can't go out at all
Today am I too young or am I too old?
No matter what I don't fit the mold

Am I too dumb or am I too smart?
How come I can never get the part?
Don't look at me, I know you will laugh
Cuz either I'm too thin or I'm too fat

You're not staring at me cuz you like what you see
I know I'm a freak and you're laughing at me
I want a perfect body, so I can be it
Tired of crying because I'm the misfit

People say beauty is on the inside
Sometimes I just wish that I would die
Cuz no one's looking there to find me
Guess I'll just have to wait and see

I want to be pretty, I want to be fine
I want you to see me and make you mine
I want to turn your head in a crowd
Can you see past the outside, can you see me at all?
Cuz the inside ain't really ugly at all

Send Me Someone

I have such a perfect life
Family, friends, success are mine
Have toys galore and even more
All the trappings to pass my time
Happiness should be mine to the core

Painted smile that hides the truth
Life's in control right on target
Strength to carry all since my youth
Everyone needs me I am always there
Where are the arms for me, when I need care?

The room is full of talking heads
People talk at me, can't hear a word
Laughing, joking the time of your life
All the people yet I am so alone
Pain sets in sharp as a knife

Need to be held it's more than I can take
Need to find that one person to embrace
Who will carry my burden when I need a break?
Who will give me that safe place to fall?
That person who will love me and take it all

Standing alone I can't feel the ground
Someone please claim me from the Lost & Found
Please send me someone to take me from the cold
And give me a place where my heart can unfold
Please send me someone, please, please, please

Ruined

When our eyes meet blue to green
Touch to touch is heat to heat
Feel your breath in my hair
I smell your scent in the cool night air
I cannot move, I do not dare

Kisses so tender like floating on air
Slowly urgent passion comes pouring through
The consequence of this night, I do not care
The fire is within and my body needs you
Together as one and all hell breaks loose

Play these chords to your hearts content
The music now comes to its intent
Hands perfect, play my body's song
Desire takes over – follow along
Arms so strong my fears are gone
Make it last forever – wait and see

The thunder I hear is somehow within
Two bodies and hearts melted together
Pull me closer and closer this must last forever
Something so beautiful cannot be a sin
This our private world, do not let it end

I'm ruined for another there is no use
I'm ruined forever, no one else but you

How did this happen, I was caught off guard
How did this happen, I have fallen so hard

I am no good for another, you are the one
I will love you forever, you are the one
I love you, I love you, you're the only one
I'm ruined forever, you're the only one

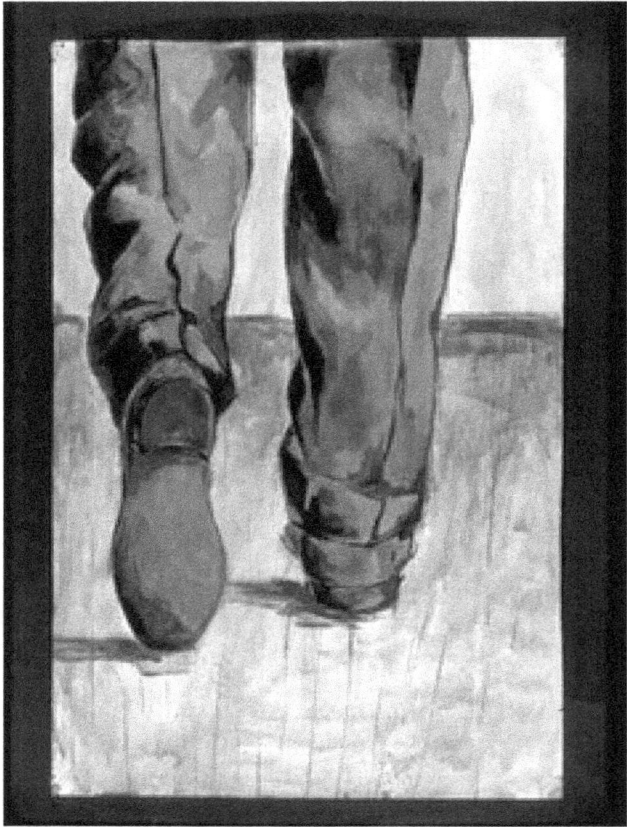

Don't Look Back

She said I'm not the man she loved before
She said I'm not the guy that she bargained for
I'm stuck in time and can't let go
This is so like her, an all time low

I keep tripping on what's in front of me
Cuz I'm looking back, won't let it be
My head keeps telling me to look ahead
Keep looking back and you'll end up dead

How can I accept that I've lost control?
She stole my heart and touched my soul
I must go on and accept my fate
Look to the future before it's too late

You will always have a place in my heart
But I need to make a brand new start
This is the last dance for you and me
I'll take control and set you free

Don't look back it's not your fault
Don't look back feelings do assault
I can't see what's in front of me
Remove these shackles and set me free

Flying with Angels

Dear Angel – thank you for being there
I always thought that I was alone
You held me up in my hour of despair
Did he send you to save me? I don't know

I wept and cried, said that love had died
You said oh no, I was simply lost
In my life I need much, much more
You said ah yes, but can you pay the price?

This pedestal of yours is too high for me
Those nice words you said, I cannot stand
I'm not that perfect, why can't you see?
You smiled at me and held out your hand

The clouds have cleared, I see the sky
Could have lost what I hold so dear
Thanks for taking me the road so high
Thank him for sending you to walk with me

Flying with angels to the edge of the earth
Feathers so soft, they comfort the hurt
Lift me to heaven it's so clear up high
Tranquility, stability, love cannot deny
Never again will I doubt my own faith
He sent me an angel, it was not too late

Wake Love

Mourn the loss forget tomorrow
Mourn the loss cloaked in sorrow
Bury your feelings that's how it goes
Say goodbye and throw a red rose

Say a prayer for the dearly departed
Suck it up, the broken hearted
Love is fragile and dies too soon
I sit quietly my brain to gloom

Dust to dust – the end has come
Ashes to ashes – loves death is here
Dust to dust – nowhere to run
Ashes to ashes – please clouds do clear

He took my hand said it would be ok
Then held me close – survive the day
It's ok to cry, the tears do not fight
Death of love always begets twilight

Wake lost love – don't be a coward
A single mourner in a silent hour
Take care the heart forever broken
Hope for new love, words not yet spoken

Dust to dust – the end has come
Ashes to ashes – loves death is here
Dust to dust – nowhere to run
Ashes to ashes – please clouds do clear

The Story Teller

Storyteller, Storyteller take me with you
To places we both can feel
Take me to comfort, take me to pain
Show me how we're both the same

It's no big deal, but a few small words
Like a drug seeping through my veins
Use them to seduce me, charm me, maybe steal
Storyteller, spin your magic – please make me feel

Stories of truth as seen through your eyes
Pain, agony, control – I feel them too
Never a laugh, I only hear your cries
Lost love, lost way, hope you find them soon

Engage me, uncage me, with deep dark secrets
Spin me up, take me down, with no regret
Stole my heart and invaded my dreams
Am I a bit player in your master scheme?

Feelings so deep, so pure – I lose my breath
Bury the pain, let's put it to death
I now know how sadness and love sound
Define your own future and turn it up loud

Do I really love you or the haunting tales?
How can one man collect so many lost souls?
Perhaps it's just a dream, you're not at all real

Perhaps this is how you want me to feel

Engage me, uncage me, with deep dark secrets
Spin me up, take me down, with no regret
Stole my heart and invaded my dreams
Am I a bit player in your master scheme?

Storyteller, Storyteller sing me your song
Storyteller, Storyteller take me along
Fill my heart and fill my soul
Make me love your rock n' roll

The Transition

2007 was the year I learned many important lessons. I learned how to be happy when life is bombarded with chaos, pain, and tragedy. I learned that when you shed your armor, amazing and wonderful things find there way into your life. I made new friends and began to allow myself time for fun. I learned there is nothing on this earth that could extinguish my love for My Warrior. It was also the year that my White Knight and I were to come to know each other. The events of 2007 changed the course of my life forever.

Insane Love

Have you ever loved someone to the end of insanity?
Felt them so deeply your soul won't stay quiet
Your heart won't be still and races through the night
And your skin hurts at those thoughts of delight

Have you ever loved someone and don't know why
They are not the best for you, not the best mate
Sometimes they forget you, they're not always there
It's not good – you know – but somehow don't care

Have you ever been addicted to that one special person?
That usual good sense would send you running
But that amazing kiss sends your brain careening
And those arms, so perfect, a heavenly feeling

Love them hard, love them fast
Take it all in while it lasts
Don't be scared, you'll lose your chance
Insane love is a gift for you
A gift that comes to but a few

Lemon

I'm sorry to them for messing up
I know you're disappointed
I need to get my act together
All your plans ruined, I'll try to do better

I'm sorry to her for keep forgetting
I know you think I am perfect
Why didn't I do this and why didn't I do that
I should have met your expectations

I'm sorry to him for asking too much
I just wanted to give happiness
Create big smiles and warm hearts
Shouldn't have asked you to take part

I'm sorry to the world, I'm not that perfect
Never pretended to be
I just want to live a good life
I just want to be free to be me

Out of My Head

You're a chronic habit in my head
A constant reminder of what's gone wrong
An uninvited guest, you crash my thoughts
Turn my dreams into disturbing scenes

Why do you torture me with your presence?
And remind me of times long lost
All the delights I can no longer enjoy
Your presence is a mindless decoy

Please leave my head and don't return
Please don't talk to me in my dreams
Don't hold me, kiss me, make me smile
Don't comfort me even for a while

I want you to disappear this very moment
Bid me a lasting farewell
I need some peace and time to forget
Missed things that are no longer mine

In my head, who put you there?
In my head, get out right now
You're not helping to solve a thing
A phantom that is driving me insane

I Miss You

I had a pleasant surprise today
A long lost feeling found its way
Into my heart, into my mind
I miss you, really, really miss you

Days go by without you here
An empty feeling of despair
How did this feeling find its way?
In our sea of trauma, day to day

I'm really sad we're far apart
But so happy I feel this way
It has been a long, long time
Since our distance felt like a crime

We've come so far on this ride
I hope our dreams don't collide
I hope we can right the wrong
And dance the dance and sing the song

I know it can never be the same
All the tears, all the pain
I pray that we can find new bliss
And seal our deal with a beautiful kiss

Blank Slate

I feel nothing, so why so many tears?
I am so sad to realize my very worst fears
You were so important, so strong and true
You're a blank slate, I'm coming unglued

I delayed this day for a very long time
You saved my life, you seemed so kind
I didn't want to arrive, feared this painful outcome
You're just a blank slate, I'm coming undone

The problem isn't you, it is definitely me
The valley of disconnect is plain to see
My emotions fly high, yours are none
Like feeding a black hole, who's coming undone

What happened to you to make you this way?
Were you ever happy until some sad day?
Now today you are a dark, blank slate
Like your soul died went to heaven's gate

The problem with idols, they are not real
The problem with me is you made me feel
What is your problem? There is nothing there
I wish I felt nothing but I still really care

It hurts so bad – you did everything right
It hurts so bad – the tears I fight
But I can't go back to before I met you
Maybe the pain is seeing you come unglued

Sad Eyes

Peering through the windows to your soul
Always open can't close the door
Hidden deep in those crystal blues
They tell your story you've paid your dues

Beautiful, beautiful sweet man
I see the tears on your sleeve
Your soul aches, your heart cries
Stole my heart those amazing sad eyes

Hard to look it makes me weep
Beautiful sweet man I'm right here
We'll find the key to set you free
Would be such a sin to end up like me

Forever your secret's safe with me
Why did this happen, I can't imagine why
I want to hold you take your hand
Help you transcend to a happy man

Grand illusions I know what's real
Can't fool me I know the deal
Heal that painful deep, deep wound
So you can feel and love real soon

Sad so deep no one can see
Sad so deep can't hide from me
Can't fool me I have traveled that road
Always here, now and forever more

Call Me

On days when life seems so cruel
When lonely and sadness seem to rule
When no one wants to give you thought
All you want is a moment caught

Turn slowly left and look inside
I am right there in your heart
To hold you, touch you, give an ear
Just punch those numbers
I'll be there

Call me, call me
I'm here for you
Dial that phone
They'll put you through
Call me, call me
Baby, always for you
Call me, call me I love you

That sunny, cold day in December
Our first hug
I'll always remember
I made a promise I plan to keep
To love you til the end of time
Protect you and keep you safe
You are my bright star
My ray of hope

So beautiful child

My shining star

Remember no matter where you are

I am always with you til the end of eternity

Never alone, always with me

Call me, call me

I'm here for you

Dial that phone

They'll put you through

Call me, call me

Baby, always for you

Call me, call me I love you

First Kiss

It was just a twist of fate
When we met on that autumn day
Two lost souls not wanting to be alone
Our fate forever changed in magical ways

We talked and shared our sad, sad tales
Of lost love that somehow derailed
Two broken hearts looking for the potion
To dull the senses and kill that emotion

Your gentle lips brushed mine so soft
With eyes closed so easy to get lost
Like a soft wave on a summers day
Lost in heaven, I wanted to stay

Softly touching your beautiful face
Not sure how you fell out of grace
Those blue, blue eyes looking at me
Those strong arms, a safe place to be

Who knew our fate was sealed that day
We never parted – never went our own way
We would kiss those sweet kisses a million times more
And love each other to heaven's door

Dear God

He should be gone you tried so hard
That deadly disease you hid so well
I did not stop and found it in time
You can't take him – he's still mine

You broke his body and his handsome face
Did you think that would stop me?
From loving his quite perfect heart
His gentle soul and all his genuine parts

You stole his mind but I have his heart
I will fight you with all that I have
Why are you trying to tear us a part
You can't take him – I won't let you

You stifled his breath, I gave him mine
Why must you commit this heinous crime?
To steal this man so loved, why?
I will fight you – you can't take him

So you left me with this broken stranger
But I still have his heart
You gave us this pure gift of love
Dear God, I beg, don't take that part

I know you always win in the end
But I can't stop – I won't give in
I know your powers are stronger than mine
But I will fight for him until the end of time - Amen

Afffnity

What mysterious energy brings us together?
Like a lost coin to a magnet
What force could draw kindred souls here?

Did this beautiful spirit will the legions to his snare?
Then hypnotize, anesthetize and energize
Just by looking into his seductive eyes

Does he have the power to keep us?
Or has another force emerged?
Do I detect a more powerful affinity?
Designed to embrace you and me

This new power is contagious
I think he has caught it too
Slowly seeping into his brain
No doubt, he will never be the same

So what is this affinity, this binding glue?
Listen closely my friend I will share with you
It is the power of giving and the grace to receive
It is the power of caring and the birth of creativity

Affinity to total strangers
What could make more sense?
Affinity of people to love, help, and defend

We will always be his subjects there is no doubt about that
Brothers and sisters joining forces giving our all with no remorse

Come Back

Where did you go, where are you now?
Why did you leave in that desperate hour?
With no warning, you left me for good
Why this happened, I never understood

I want to see you and love you so bad
Those brilliant blue eyes staring at me
I want to hold you and keep you near
And whisper little secrets in your ear

Come back and kiss me, it's not a crime
Come back and hold me one more time
My eyes are leaking from thoughts of you
My heart is twisted, my love so true

I wasn't ready to say goodbye
I called and called but no reply
I wasn't prepared for what I found
You lying so still on that cold, cold ground

They brought you back, or so they said
To rise again from the dead
They saved your body, but not your mind
Please come hold me just one more time

Come back to me, I miss you
Come back to me, I love you
I love you, I love you, please come back
I love you, I love you, please come back

Fake

You're such a fake, you're such a joke
You've got them fooled, it makes me choke
Poor little thing says feel sorry for me
Poor little thing, as helpless as can be

So what is behind this meek little act?
A helpless dwarf kitten or a sly tiger cat?
A picture so clear, so why does no one see?
I don't really care, cuz it's not about me

Lost love, oh I think not
Intentions are seen and scary as hell
Your words and eyes are so clear
You're on the hunt bringing your prey near

I hope no one gets hurt in your devious little scheme
I wish you goodwill, but the truth must be told
A piece of flawed glass, not a precious gem
Be true to yourself, and do not hurt him

Matters of the Heart

It seemed like a lifetime ago
When love burned beyond control
A fire so hot it scorched your breath
Bright flame never put to death

But matters of the heart are a bit tricky
Sometimes what was becomes our sad history
Your door slammed shut, heart locked tight
Ice fortress built to survive long, lonely nights

You have tried every lethal elixir and potion
To relieve that dark and painful emotion
You wonder why you're stuck in this place
The future seems like an unlit, endless maze

You have been in cold storage for so long
Do you remember when hearts were warm?
The time has come to find the key
Melt the ice, open your heart and set it free

In matters of the heart I have learned
Unconditional love is the only truth
Everything else is a dead end game
Results always a short lived flame

So my friend, I tell you true
Open your heart and get your due
Look deep and let love into your heart
You can love again, it is time to start

Bad Guy

Don't want to be the bad guy any more
Broken fingers when you slam the door
Never bargained for unbridled wrath
Aimed straight at me you hit the gas

I only say what others think
Whispering secrets into space
They want to catch a shining star
I want the star to shine forever

I could play the game like all the rest
Praises galore, you are the best
An easy path, a smooth, silky ride
Let the star burn out and finally die

It's not who I am, I am sorry to say
I want to have fun, I want to play
But I need to stand and tell you true
I will fight shining star, just for you

So see me as you will
So see me as you might
What will you do now?
Will you stand up and fight?

Deafening Silence

So tell me, were the stars too bright?
Blinding yet another lonely night
Where has the forever party gone?
Is this silence too loud for you?

They told you so very, very perfect
No need to check your compass
Shoot the flagman, just an annoyance
Can you hear the silence in that deep trance?

Let's blame him, her, and them
Hide in the basement and pretend
That the skies remain crystal clear
And that there is nothing to fear

One way streets always have an end
No way back, did I think you a friend?
Perhaps I was just a wind up toy
To pass some time and make some noise

Spite is a sharp and a dangerous weapon
Yes, you really showed us all
It's a gift to be in the king's presence
But I ask again, is the silence deafening?

A prisoner in your own castle
No visitors allowed

Permission

It unfolded like a tragic love story
Two bodies always needing to embrace
Hot steamy kisses yearning to discover
Private touches, the desire to please the other

Then like a thief lurking in the shadows
With stealth and finesse it snatched our bliss
Extinguished our hot fire of together
And sweet times we thought would last forever

My love, it left you diminished without depth
And me a horrid, ugly, empty mess
I was not brave enough to see our future
Anesthesia seemed my perfect solution

I traveled the earth in my secret coma
Each day adding layers of disgrace
Then a handsome knight appeared in a vision
And said, "Choose hope, I give permission"

I discarded the poisons that numbed my whole being
Stood straight and looked in the mirror
A stranger looked back with sad, lonely eyes
To her I said "Run, don't stop, I give permission"

I ran and ran and shed my disgrace
Chastised myself for lost time what a waste
The knight reappeared and said "It's time, come see me"

"I will give you a gift to set laughter free"

I went and met this mysterious man
He held me, laughed, and gave me his hand
Again I looked at the stranger in the mirror
And said "Laugh, don't stop, I give permission"

I ran and laughed and met new friends
My love, I saw you laughing too
Now the person looking back in the mirror is me
Saying "Choose happy, it's alright, it's permitted"

There is but one issue that I cannot resolve
The battle between honor and need
My knight whispered "Life could be good if you let it"
But confusion remains, can I really permit it?

.

Hunger

My journey is of discovery
Destination unknown
Paths so many, for me, not all lead to Rome
My taste craves what is different
Sameness does not appeal to me
Experiment and learn is to be set free

I wandered down a path discovering a foreign land
Nothing felt familiar my heart began to pound
Yes, an intriguing place with such delightful sounds
A stranger turned my way he did not look like me
Our differences so many just so plain to see
Hmmm, I was hungry instantly

He spoke an ancient dialect to my ears long forgot
Just a few words filled with meaning
Rats, no subtitles for me to read
The words felt cruel, so I chose to fight
In fact his words were only to entice
The gates then lowered quickly my passage denied

With differences so many and so much to be learned
I wonder if it was sameness this exotic man did yearn
Too bad, experimentation would have interested me
I am saddened by this outcome
But must continue my quest
Hunger compels me, I cannot come to rest

Dark Heart

So many lovers yet no one to love
So much attention yet always alone
Your choices are so many
Yet you choose to trust no one

What happened that you built such a thick wall?
With chains on the door no lights in the hall
Did someone do battle with your sweet, tender heart
Leaving scars so deep you hide in the dark

You have tried every elixir and deadly potion
To relieve that dark and painful emotion
Such a deep wound that just will not heal
Bury the truth it's too hard to feel

It's so hard to watch, so hard to see
Such a beautiful person as lonely as can be
Sadness so deep branding your soul
So guarded against shadows, it's taken a toll

I offer my hand to show you the way
Turn on the lights, shine on a new day
Nothing in return for you are quite special
We all deserve love; these wounds are not fatal

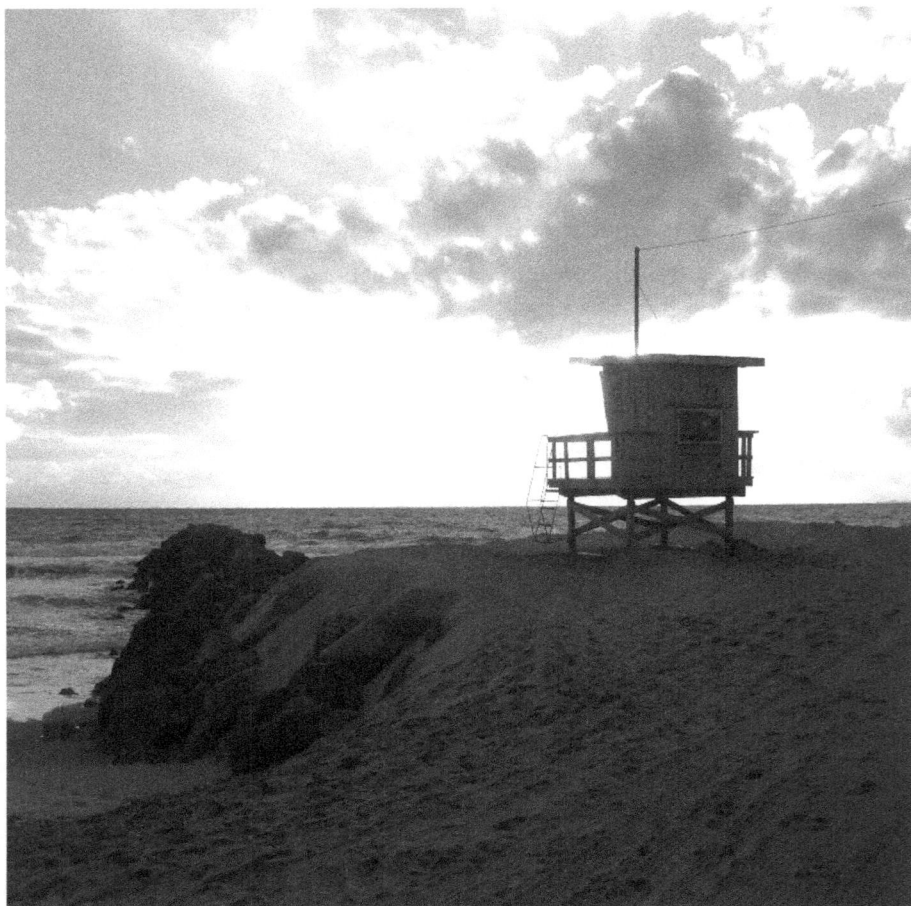

Sanctuary

This beautiful still night
I have finally reached my sanctuary
Where sun, sand, and sea collide
I close my eyes to quiet my mind

The heavy scent of salt in the air
My nightly walk from pier to pier
My saving grace from insanity
Each night lifting me up to set me free

So many faces, yet all alone
Each sense slowly comes alive
Inhale slowly, see water and stars touch, feel sand, taste the salty air
It is so easy to forget these heavenly things, with life's daily haste

I wonder how many are on the same quest
To relish each moment with no regrets
A rose in the garden along the way
I stop, look, smell, touch the silky petals

My perfect sanctuary

Choices

It was such a long time ago
I still remember your face so clearly
You came at such an inopportune time
When bells and vows were soon to be mine

The connection was instant
A force neither could deny
So apparent to all around us
My confused heart - no answers to trust

Tall and handsome, baby blue eyes
Solid as stone, walked a straight line
Legs that went on forever and ever
Oh lord, my weakness, that is for sure

It would have been a better fit
Than the crazy, insane place that I was in
Safer and stronger, and did I mention those limbs
Suddenly my direction looked dark and grim

Why did you arrive at the eleventh hour?
Was I being tested or just a coward?
Tried to quiet that pesky little voice
Can't hurt your love, you have no choice
Life is full of hard choices
Some more difficult than others
That's what makes life so interesting
Often just a choice – no right or wrong, that's the thing
Oh yea, I chose insanity – No regrets

Nowhere

What the hell is wrong with me?
School girl thought won't let me be
There's no real reason to feel this way
Is good sense in a mood to betray?
The truth is I feel a little bit stung
Not even an honorable mention
Did you think it so ridiculous?
It's already tossed in the recycle box

It's not the first time such a reminder
Came to visit to set me straight
I am just an uninvited guest
Allowed short visits with the rest

You've done nothing wrong, just being yourself
This foolishness is my entire fault
Never been cool, not trying to be
Just want to fit in and still be me

Insecurity is a foreign disease
I hate how it makes me bleed
In my world I stand strong with might
Your world turns me small and trite

It is only fitting that you're the one
To make me see I don't belong
This time, last time, the time before
Did you laugh when I showed up at the door?

I will not go back to that dead place
Where emptiness rules the entire day
So if I do not belong here
Then I ask where?   Nowhere.

Normal

There was a time in my life
When I craved for normalcy
To have the car, the spouse, the home
To mirror what was around me

I heard the words at every turn
About this steady place
Where my life looks just like yours
Yesterday, today, tomorrow on repeat

Very young this reflection is imprinted on our souls
Normal defines us with every lesson told
It is who we are and how we are judged
By you and them and me

The truth is what is normal and is unique for you and me
Born with knowledge in our hearts put there for us to see
Normal is how we define ourselves and stay on our own course
Normal changes every moment as we grow and live and learn

Some people learn this lesson when they are young and strong
Others stay the course imprinted and wonder what went wrong
I learned this lesson late, but not to late to change my ways
Today I live my life with a new normal every day

Light

The darkness claimed its victory for a very long time
Day after day the stillness with no end was mine
Then without warning a distant speck of light appeared
Flickering through the darkness making destiny unclear

It's a choice to remain a statue in the night
Or dare to take even a tiny step into the light
Letting sadness and fear guide the way
Will tarnish the soul at the end of the day

How long will this new light shine?
Just a moment or till the end of time
In the end it matters not
Be brave, catch the light and give it a shot

Experience the magic of the dancing light
Slowly making its way to the surface
It has been a long time coming
It is breathtaking

Roller Coaster Ride

Hold on tight I feel it climbing
One notch at a time
In slow motion climbing high
Air so thin euphoria the prize

Up, up high in the sky
Down, down lower than ground
Love me or leave me
I like it this way
Love me or leave me
Don't judge me today

Top of the world
Frenetic frenzy no sleep required
Moving too fast to see any gray
Brilliance, laughter mine each day

Like the scary amusement park ride
Highs so high, lows so low
Strapped in tight
Else fall forever out of sight
My life's a rollercoaster ride
I like it that way
Strapped in so tight
Else forever out of sight

Up, up high in the sky
Down, down lower than ground

Love me or leave me
I like it this way
Love me or leave me
Don't judge me today

Crash, crash crashing hard
Crash crash don't look down
Crash crash crashing hard
Crash crash don't hit the ground

Sadly for every high there comes a low
Feeling it slip away here we go
Descending faster than the speed of light
Into the depths of fog and dark night

Air is thick all sounds distant and muffled
Movement optional, sleep preferred
Hold on tight soon to be rising
One notch at a time

Up, up high in the sky
Down, down lower than ground
Love me or leave me
I like it this way
Love me or leave me
Don't judge me today

Crash, crash crashing hard
Crash crash don't look down
Crash crash crashing hard
Crash crash don't hit the ground

Indian Summer

I know I am ancient
As old if not older than dirt
My reflection tells no lies
I've roamed this earth for a while

I've traveled to lands far and wide
Experienced some of life's finest desserts
My trophies are many and quite divine
Some say luck – perhaps - but more likely it was hard work

I've accomplished so much – yet it seems so little
How many more journeys do I have?
I feel like I am just getting started
If my choice - - this quest will never end

My heart is filled with so much passion and hope
My soul yearns for a million times more
The ones who look like me have declared themselves done
Those that dream like me perceive their too young

Such a quandary perhaps there is no answer
I'm stuck between the beginning and end
Maybe I'll find someone who sees many dimensions
With the wisdom and desire to cherish Indian Summer

Foolish Girl

We all have fears that set our direction
Some fear rejection so won't give their heart
Others fear failure and never make a start
My fear is to be seen as a foolish girl

Extraordinary measures have been spent
To block all holes in this dam
And plaster the cracks in every wall
No one would ever suspect I could slip or fall

I am so very cautious with matters of men
Always taking care not to embarrass me or them
I assume the chosen ones are not attracted
To a plain woman with no shiny facets

So I use humor and laughter
To hide my insecurity
Certainly most men would never want me
Never, ever to be ridiculed as a fool

Yet if a prince came calling how would I know
My barricade is a fortress – no one gets in
I would not believe his preference is me
Foolish girl

Truth and Hope

This is the story of truth and hope
Where two unlikely worlds collide
One needed to see truth to face life
The other full of hope hitting his stride

Combustible energy with cute hat tricks
And stylish clothes an interesting mix
Not even close to my preferred cup of tea
Not bad - but you didn't convince me

I paid little attention until you stood still
And revealed your soul through your voice
And then graced us with that amazing smile
Spellbound, you took my breath away

Each week was an amazing event
You became the art rather than the performance
I want to experience you again and again
And now feel so privileged that you call me friend

So many women proclaim their love for you
I never thought it possible to love a stranger
Still not sure if my heart has made an exception
But I do care beyond my comprehension

The truth is I'm addicted to your brain
Thoughts so complex, I cannot refrain
Your world is a mosaic of intricate contrasts

You the teacher, I the student – inverse roles cast

In the end you are simply a man
With wishes and hopes and dreams
You probably enjoy long, intimate hugs
Like everyone else just want to be loved

So on this day and special occasion
I give you the simplest of gifts
You have my heart, my smile, my wish
That love finds you and you find it.

Light of Day

The sun is rising once again
Blinding my tired eyes
For sleep this night is not to be mine
A night fraught with secrets and crimes

As the light of day penetrates my brain
I ponder whether I will ever be the same
For the demons of the evening stole my being
Showed me sins that left me wounded and seething

With the blackness of night giving no compass
I swung my weapon in all directions
Blindly striking at ghosts in demon attire
Not knowing if collateral damage ensued in the cross fire

But as the rays of this day shine on my sad face
I ponder who the victim and now sit in disgrace
For often wolves hide in lamb's wool
And cleverly snare the prey easily fooled

Perhaps the lamb was the demon in disguise
And the demon innocent although not very wise
And I again a fool who does not belong here
Insecurity my wound that continues to bleed

Under Siege

The year started and ended with battles happening on every front. It felt like there was never one moment to exhale and relax. My warrior endured multiple fights for his life, my white knight was in major transition during the summer and fall, and I continued to struggle in the workplace. 2008 was a challenge to say the least.

I spent the year feeling like I was frozen in place. I had made so much progress in the previous two years I was really hard on myself about it. What I eventually came to understand that year was that sometimes standing still is the very best that a person can do and a major accomplishment when sliding backwards can be such an easy choice.

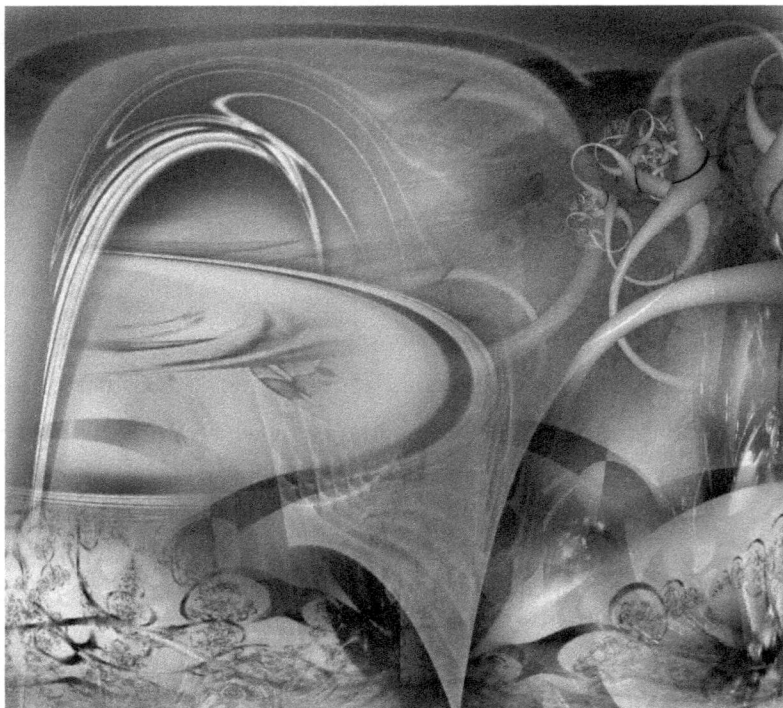

Connect

It's not a mystery what life's about
It is to make connections, there's little doubt
Some need to create tidy symmetrical spider webs
Mine is more like a cosmic symphony

There are countless dimensions to my divine creation
Endless pure energy exploding to fruition
Come with me, let's take time to touch
Differences pure magic – for me what it's all about

Touching a life will make a change in direction
The connection can be a kaleidoscope of cosmic creation
When you let it unfold with no set expectations
It can take you to places of unsurpassed pleasure and elation

There are connections that hurt and burn like hell
But if you don't try and touch them there is no way to tell
Others will kindle that hot flame in your heart
Connected forever – never apart

I dare to be different, I dare to be me
Such an unlikely connection, that set me free
Wish I knew and hope soon there's enough trust
To tell me the other side, tell me the rest

I can only hope that I give more than I receive
And my connection touches you and makes you believe
Be brave let all the connections turn on
Feel the good, the bad, and far, far beyond

The Peacock the Scarecrow and the Rose

There once was a Rose that lived in the woods
She loved with all her heart and tried to be good
Rose had a huge resolve but not a large stature
Sweet on the outside but tenacious in nature

One day a handsome peacock strutted by looking cool
She wanted him bad that is all Rose knew
His bright lovely feathers were enticing and fine
She thought to herself this peacock will be mine

Well the peacock was loud and full of himself
And treated Rose with callous unlike everyone else
His flamboyant style attracted many fine ladies
But it was other crimes that drove Rose crazy

The Peacock and Rose would spend their time together
But she could not voice her words through his feathers
He looked down on whatever would please this lovely Rose
So she kept well hidden all her secrets and prose

One day Rose was wandering through the thick woods
Where sunlight and darkness fight for her mood
Rose was deep in her thoughts and not quite aware
When a creature jumped out and gave her a scare

What's this character with limbs as long as a broom?
And a funny hat that he would do better to lose
He had a gentle touch and a heart made of gold
He was the Scarecrow from Hell is what she was told

She needed to find out for herself
Whether he was good or bad or perhaps something else
Rose needed someone to share her deep darkest thoughts
He was not much to look at but she liked him a lot

Rose learned that the hens loved this electric scarecrow
So she paid him attention and learned so much more
He wanted to listen and understand intricate thoughts
He kept all her secrets undercover and locked

So the Scarecrow turned out not to be scary at all
And the Peacock ended up rather dusty and dull
Rose turned a new color and found her new voice
The Scarecrow will always be her number one choice

Roses are red
The Scarecrow is blue
The Rose and Peacock wed
But she's still thinking of you

Bittersweet

It has been a bittersweet journey these last few years
The joy of new discoveries all stained with tears
Winning each battle but losing the war
The bitter with the sweet surely settles the score

I never imagined that this story would be told
The brilliance in each day as the chapters unfold
Then each night turns to black as the truth makes its mark
Leaving sadness and sorrow to resurface in the dark

The man who knows me will never be mine
I could be sad but it just wasn't our time
The man I love will never be the same
As evil swiftly won its hateful cruel game

Strangers have surfaced to hold me up high
While my circle of love will not let me cry
I could be angry at this turn of events
But that is not how I want my story to end

Is life predetermined or random and free?
Is each day a discovery or is there really destiny?
I don't really care because I live for each moment
Hoping that sweet wins and bitter comes in a distant second

One Mile

You think you know me
I believe you are mistaken
I am not sure you have a clue
For you've never walked a mile in my shoes

Do you think that I don't bleed?
Do you even care that I have needs?
Your words hurt me, make me blue
Go ahead, try, walk a mile in my shoes

Do you listen when I share my story?
Or are you only thinking of yours?
Don't I get to have an opinion, a life?
Without being hammered with senseless strife

We are one family, why can't you see
I want to be there for you, please be there for me
You can't imagine the challenges to pay my dues
Until you've walked a mile in my shoes

The Musician

The room was a throwback from a long, long time ago
Dimly lit tables, the smell of smoke and booze stifling the air
Scattered about a few lost souls trying to drown their sorrows
With the haunting sound of a sax wailing in the background

Slowly she makes her way to that lonely barstool
And orders her favorite poison to dull all the emotions
Eyes transfixed on her half filled glass
Praying no one will attempt contact

The sultry seductive sound slowly engulfs her
And stirs ancient memories long forgotten
As if frozen in time the sax player holds her gaze
She remembers sweet times, back to those lazy, hazy days

Closing her eyes she feels the soothing notes enter
Her heart, her soul reaching deep frames within her
To a time when she could make that tenor sax cry
Her breath creating the magic, until all the ugly pain died

In those days, as is now, many liked to create labels

Just one look and they all doubted her talents
At times God seems to have such a wicked sense of humor
When she hit that first note, she would dispel all those rumors

She cannot recall why she abandoned this true love
But her life is not one of regrets
A smile slowly forms while she reminisces her favorite parts
When music lifted her soul, her true love was this art

This Moment

Breathe in slowly and let it embrace you
I'll guide you to this place of ecstasy
This paradise I have chosen for you and me

Crazy, or perhaps as wise as the day is long
Knowing the only certainty is this moment in time
Come with me and indulge in the sweet and sublime

As the grenades of fear explode all around us
Let's transcend the misery and partake in joy
Take my hand I will guide you through this door

I know tomorrow looks bleak and dreary
But remember so did this very moment in time
Let's rejoice and ignore all life's crimes

Kiss me. Smile.
What could be more important?
This precious moment

Screaming in Silence

Finally the noise of the day has subdued
As the quiet of night gradually seeps through
Dissolving my fabricated daily distractions
Revealing my endless nightmare's reflection

My mind knows the ugly truth
What is best for me may not be best for you
But my heart continues to win this battle
I cannot let go and I never will

I see you fading with each passing day
The forever battles have taken their toll
My heart is screaming its silent plea
Darling please keep fighting for you and me

Is it so selfish for me to want you to stay?
When it's so hard to exist another day
Please take everything that I have to give
I scream in silence – don't lose the will to live

I love you with all my heart
I have since the very start
Do I love you enough to will you stay?
Should I love you enough to let you go?

Do you hear me screaming in silence?
I will never accept that we are at the end
Fight with me with all that you've got
Don't leave me to drown in such an unbearable loss

Touch Me Touch You

The feel of your finger tips across my skin
Your hands caressing my face, I can barely breathe in
The room is so quiet I can hear your heart pound
I love that my closeness creates that lovely sound

Get closer I want your essence to seep through
I want to hear that delightful groan from you
Let me touch your arms, your chest, your everything
To send you to places only known in your dreams

The scent of your body makes my heart skip beats
Our bodies together make us perfectly complete
Your warmth against me sends me soaring within
Let's memorize this moment to relive again and again

Moments like these are the purest of pure
Moments to cherish forever being with you
I will always remember the best of our times
You made my world dazzle thank you for being mine

I know these moments are now a distant history
And now each day is full of only memories
But you will always have a special place in my heart
We are no longer together, but will never be apart

When I think of you I will not cry for what is lost
I will smile for the beautiful pure love that was

Touch me, touch you

Last Dance

As I walked through the room
Music was singing through the tube
Stopping in my tracks – it was our song
You took me in your arms – I was stunned it was you

Some love disappears through free will
I lost you to disease
It is bittersweet you are here but gone
Stole my breath when you remembered our song

You held me so close, so gentle
We glided across the room
I whispered in your ear "I love you"
This moment please last forever, but I knew

The music came to its final verse
I looked up into your amazing blue eyes
And there you were for just a moment
Then returned the stranger, it came to an end

In the rare precious moments
When you surface again
I am happy yet sad
Wondering will this be the last dance?

Exhale

My sweet darling, come lean on me
I have enough strength for us both
Do not worry I will make everything right
For I am fearless and promise to win this fight

Oh baby, take my hand, squeeze and hold tight
I am by your side through this dark time
Rest your eyes, take that peaceful sleep
I am fearless and there is no need to weep

Every cell in my body I have willed to steel
As I sit patiently not daring to feel
Holding my breath while I await the news
Have no fear my love, I will not let us lose

My beautiful man it is now time to exhale
We have won another battle
Rest now for tomorrow you must recover
So we can rejoice and again be together

I love you with everything I've got
Now and forever no matter what
My love, exhale, relax I will take care of the rest
Things are not perfect but I promise to do my best

Sometimes life takes many twists and turns
And the things that we had are no longer ours
Whether we are together or end up apart
You will forever have a special place in my heart

Ultimate Love

They were words I never imagined to hear
The years were always about you
Never about me
Then came that moment I could hardly believe

A lifetime of doubt has always been my crime
I never knew the depth of your love
You always held back in fear of another ugly wound
I only wanted you to love me as much as I loved you

And then it happened out of the blue
In the middle of my hectic day
You came to me and held me tight
And whispered words of the ultimate sacrifice

In a million years I never would have guessed
The depth of your strength and love
You are the bravest man on this planet
Your only concern to ensure my happiness

Although life for us took a dramatic turn
Your mind and body continue to be brutally attacked
Know this: you never, ever need to fear
I will be yours for at least the next million years

Waiting

Another waiting room, another long wait
I've come accustom to life this way
This cold, sterile place so far from home
We're at the next crisis, our next melodrome

On which day did I learn to be still?
And patiently wait for you
On which day did I decide?
To be forever by your side

The truth is you've spent a lifetime waiting for me
As I took flight to realize my dreams
Cheering me always, never letting on
Your painful loneliness while I was gone

Far too many cold empty nights
Yearning for arms to hold you tight
Picturing me alone in that hotel bed
Counting the days until we touch again

Quietly standing in the shadows
You were always there for me
Welcoming me home with that sweet, sweet smile
Never complaining I was there for such a short while

They say absence makes the heart grow fonder
Shows you what they know
Distance will either ignite or extinguish

No matter how strong or pure the love is

We are so blessed
My travels brought us even closer
Every moment cherished when together
Too often apart, but bonded forever

How lucky am I that you had the strength
To adjust your life to accommodate my dreams
Not an easy path, but we had little choice
Your support always love's strongest voice

So now it is my turn to wait for you
What could be more important right now?
I will wait for you until the end of time
My privilege to wait until you are by my side

Who's the Boss?

Has there ever been any real doubt?
What our tug of war has been all about
Is it about control or something else?
You are the boss, you have no doubt

Did you think that I didn't get the lesson?
Did you think that I was so naïve?
Perhaps I am, in a female kind of way
Yes dear, you're the boss night and day

After all, it is all about you
Such a brilliant and sensual view
I acquiesce to your every demand
Your victory speech suggests an upper hand

Although I succumb to your every wish
Does not mean my actions are without thought
It simply says that I am committed to you
Unconditionally, it's the ultimate dues

You may think that you are king of the roost
And in many ways you are
But please do not mistake my submissive actions
As anything other than my generous gift of devotion

So who's the boss? You are, of course.

Surrender

I surrender, it's no use
I've no strength to resist
The real truth is I never wanted to
You are my drug of choice

I lied to myself for a long time
That my interests were pure and simple
But I dropped my guard and you hypnotize me
Now I have no desire to be set free

So do what you will
Tell me your wishes
Share your most intimate desires
How shall we spend this time together?

Shall we talk about hopes?
And share secret dreams
Or kiss under the brilliant stars
Slowly divulging who we really are

Do you want to hold me? It's ok
I don't want to fight another day
I want to feel your weight over me
And smell your scent so fresh and clean

And touch your face and arms and legs
And share the pleasures of two
Then hold you tight for just a while

And hope I've made your heart smile

So no more riddles, please come clean
And tell me in simple terms
Just say hello, I will do the rest
Please do not leave me to guess

I do not play games, it is not my style
I just wish to give and receive
Whatever gifts you have to offer
Will be returned one thousand fold

You know where to find me
You have knocked on my door before
I promise to greet you with open arms
To you I surrender, the next step is yours

Trusted Souls

It's not fair
It's just not right
I finally found someone
Who sees me for who I really am

Someone who feels deeper than deep
And can read my feelings like a book
Someone who in a past life I would have dismissed
It's not fair I'll never even get one sweet kiss

I know my secrets are locked tight and safe
A sweet character who allows me endless mistakes
Who has given me the courage not to care
When others think I'm foolish and constantly stare

It's just not fair I can never hold him close
Spending precious moments embracing hope
How can this be right?
Never together for even one night

I guess it was just never my fate
To be with someone who cares about me that way
But I understand fairness was never life's game
I am so grateful for what I do have, just the same

I wish I may, I wish I might
Share all my secrets with you tonight
Then you'll smile and trust me too
Forever trusted souls, me and you

Chocolate

I want it, the desire I cannot deny
It has been awhile since I indulged
In one of life's finer treasures
Chocolate – my secret, guilty pleasure

I have been a good girl for such a long time
Used to be naughty – that's not such a crime
I love chocolate and have had my fair share
Enough for a whole team, but no one seemed to care

The varieties are many with no end in sight
I dream about chocolate almost every night
I want to feel its warm pleasure inside my mouth
Sweet scent assaulting until I can't get out

So silky and smooth rolling on my tongue
Ever so careful to make it last so very long
Start slowly and gently with little bites
Until I lose myself to such sensual heights

Yes, I do so love chocolate
And the pleasures it brings
The question is can I have just one
Or will I again become undone?

Dear Friend

Friendship is the gift to give and receive
We are becoming friends, I want to believe
Not fifty fifty rather one hundred one hundred
The gift to love and forgive each other

Dear friend you have my prized possession – trust
That our private words always stay between us
And you say what you mean and mean what you say
And respect my feelings at the end of the day

Dear friend you also have my precious time
Please take all that you need
I am always here to support you
Especially when we don't share the same views

Dear friend I give you the power of my mind
I will be your teacher some of the time
And your student when you take the lead
I am open to many roles with inhibitions freed

Sometimes I wonder what you want from me
I hope it is friendship not merely curiosity
I treasure you simply for the person that you are
I see you as a different kind of star

I apologize I am not skilled at silly sound bites
There is too much to be said into the night
Your moments of silence make me nervous and scared
I pray nothing is wrong you have not misinterpreted me

Please receive these gifts I have bestowed upon you
They are important gifts the binding glue
There are no conditions and certainly no strings
Unconditional friendship that's the thing

Between the Lines

Between the lines is what he said
Subtle messages he secretly read
Some do not dabble in meaningless words
Meaningless talk she never preferred

Such a rarity to share the betweens
Such a beautiful soul who gets what it means
Who is listening – who is awake?
Viewing her troubled soul's endless earthquake

So now and forever the 'tweens are for you
For there is so much that has now come due
At times others may come into view
But will be openly marked and clearly tattooed

Like a beautiful treasure hidden below
Waiting to be discovered to surface and glow
Holding many secrets seldom revealed
The hunt is for the master to unconceal

Beauty comes in many unique forms
And some connections are outside the norm
Peel back the layers there is much to share
Leap of faith to the 'tweens only if you dare

The Experiment

I just love a brand new experiment
Discovery is my guilty pleasure
Willing to try can never fail
Failure is plodding along the same old trail

Discovery feeds my soul
And taught me about faith and beyond
Laugh at me if you will
But my life is an amazing never ending thrill

Those who proclaim to hold all the answers
Have already arrived at the end
Repetition numbs their long dull minutes
Its ok, they'll never be part of my experiment

I've been watching you for quite a while
Were you looking for a magic answer?
Tell me again, what was the question?
Please stop thinking and go discover something

Life's most amazing discoveries
Were found by those willing to try
So please baby, what are you waiting for?
I promise, you'll find gems you weren't looking for

And if you should get lost along the way
Grab onto my hand - always here to stay
So don't go down that path where you've been before
Take a deep breath, just go, there's an amazing new world to explore

In and Out

In for the journey, destination unknown
Outcome perhaps connections are born

In for the joy to discover many layers
To learn, grow and dare to be there

Venture through the door to see the other side
No tolls required passage allowed

Bring an intriguing harvest to the table
A feast for those who choose and are able

Not seeking the revered shiny gold medal
No interest in the weight of heavy trinkets

To stand with others in the army of faith
Be alive, be present, no time to waste

To extend a hand when others are lost
To extend a voice no matter the cost

So what is the desired outcome of all this?
The sublime pleasure to love and to give

Soaring

I sit here indulging in the comfort of this quiet night
My brain still spinning from the madness and chaos
Wounds of the day continue to bleed
As I try to steady my head and struggle to breathe

Beautiful white knight you appeared one dark summer's eve
We began our forever journey or so I believed
Have we arrived at the final destination or simply switching planes?
For me there can be no end – I couldn't endure that pain

Standing still was never our destiny
No choice but to fly high for you and for me
Forever to venture into the clouds of the unknown
Compelled to soar, risking it all, will we fall or will we drown?

Beautiful white knight as I watch you leap and fly away
I am reminded that I am standing still and here I cannot stay
My eyes are leaking I will not remain stuck by poisonous glue
I will dust off my ragged wings and take flight to soar with you

Naked

Open the door and come on through
Your amazing life patiently waits for you

Open your eyes let the brilliant light in
The time has come to shed old skin

Open your heart and embrace loves touch
Give freely and the returns will be so much

Live and love with everything you've got
Don't hold back or you'll miss a lot

Laugh and smile, live in the moment
These simple things render pure enjoyment

Beautiful soul, reveal yourself to the world
And fear not how circumstances unfold

Sweet tender heart it is time to trust again
Let happiness in to be your friend

Locking in the pain and uncertainty
Also locks out all hope and how the future can be

Get naked and let the world see the truth
There is no other way for me and for you

Teacher

Teacher, teacher what's the word?
I'm looking at you cuz I want to learn
Where are the books, where is the board?
Teach me something new I'm insanely bored

I have been studying hard to learn all the rules
But they're so complex I need some clues
I know part of the lesson is to figure it out
But at times leaves me frustrated and full of doubt

Each day I anxiously hurry to your special class
Cuz you are looking good and one real bad a**
It is fun to play pranks and break all the rules
So I can be in detention with you after school

Teacher, teacher it is time to get started
Everyone's laughing cuz Dan just farted
He thinks he's the cool captain, oh give me a break
The only thing he can charm is a bunch of sorry snakes

I want to learn cool stuff and have some fun
And play until normal has come all undone
So let's get started, please show me the new lesson
Cuz I am eager to get going and tired of guessing

Covers

They say you can't judge a book by its cover
I once thought this true but now begin to wonder
I've realized that the extremes are where truth is veiled
What meets the eye provides clues to the true tale

We all make decisions on the design of our cover
What we want to display and reveal to one another
Like a book with a complex story to tell
Our covers display what we are hoping to sell

Some go to extremes to sculpt their bodies to perfection
And dress to please and turn heads in their direction
Their mask is a vision of beauty but what is within
Perhaps trying to hide dark secrets under their skin

Look at me look at me is their daily mantra
But they only want you to see their outside sparkle
They are always the one chosen, the ones who get in
But secretly fear discovery of the monster within

Others choose a much larger or colorless disguise
That burdens their bodies to hide what they despise
They wear tents for garments and sulk in the dark
And skulk through the world not leaving a mark

The larger they get the more invisible they become
And relish the idea no one sees them undone
They hate the person that lays hidden within

And think that their cover can bury their sins

I have observed and know all these things to be true
But these covers are not always the rule
Some people's covers tell the whole truth
The inside and outside match perfectly through

The lesson here is you can often tell a book by its cover
Extreme covers may try to hide what's down under
It is not always designed to give the world a clue
So tell me what does your cover say about you?

Evil

Evil showed its ugly face today
With those sinister eyes glaring our way
I still myself trying to comprehend
Not knowing the beginning or the end

I may have been caught at a time
When life's sentinel was not mine
Did you think that I was so awestruck?
And too naïve to figure it out

I have news for you
You were wrong, very, very wrong
And now monster, you are forever gone

You did not count on the real connection
It was not all your sick fantasy
You did not count on good prevailing
Two bright stars united and shining

I know that evil sometimes wins
This time good ensured no life scars
I know that the universe has a way
Of reconciling deeds on judgment day

Know this to be true
I will not rest
Until the day is here
When your evil is extinguished forever

True Beauty

Have you ever wanted someone regardless of their looks?
Or must they resemble pretty dolls in pretty picture books
Have you ever met someone whose beauty is revealed?
Only after time and closeness worked their appeal

Is your only interest what pleases your eye?
Do you even check what is on the inside?
Is party hard the only priority?
Does someone's depth count for anything?

Have you ever noticed that when a person touches your heart
You soon can't turn away from their engaging smile
Their eyes begin to look so perfect and bright
You want to hold on to their beauty through the night

I ask these questions of myself and everyone
Because what pleases our senses may not see us through
To keep safe and secure our souls and our hearts
And hold us when our earthquakes measure off the charts

It may be too late for me I have made serious mistakes
And followed a path of attraction until it was too late
He was a handsome man with such shallow thoughts
It was never about me, I was always forgot

Do you dare to be different do you dare to be brave?
And stay with someone who your eye may not crave
But warms your tender heart and safeguards your troubled soul

And will be strong for you and never throw you to the cold

Because true beauty will shine its perfect face
And comes from the inside with dignity and grace
And one day you will wonder what was wrong
When your brain could not see their perfection all along

Last Laugh

She sits alone pondering events
That forced a change in direction
For a thief in disguise stole something dear
There is no mistake his intentions now clear

Only natural to feel angry, sad, and hurt
But these emotions seem to elude her
Could it be joy and laughter I hear?
Has the girl gone mad, realizing her worst fears?

An artist driven by love, passion, and desire
Fame, fortune, greed absent from her repertoire
Her art a complex blend of science and imagination
The results must be cloaked – top secret creations

When driven by passion rather than fortune and fame
The prize is measured in the art, not the coins
Fame self declared, safely tucked in her heart
Impossible to steal, impossible to stop

Ignorant man - you seek only fame and fortune
Good luck with those hollow goals
You only destroyed the brushes, not the artist
Blinded by bright lights you can't discern the difference

You simply inflicted a small wound - nothing fatal
For no one can steal her dreams and passion
She will find a new path to fulfill her needs
His future in doubt only driven by greed

Kiss Kiss

So you think I don't have a mind of my own
Should be a cynic like you wearing that frown
I have two words for you – Kiss Kiss

You know nothing of the path that I take
You assume your path is the only way
To you I say – Kiss Kiss

Pretending to be something you're not
Beguiling mask, I hope he has doubts
Careful there – Kiss Kiss

Things are not always as they appear
Two faces should always live in fear
Sooner or later – Kiss Kiss

I get him, we're connected for life
I will stand by him through all the senseless strife
As for you – Kiss Kiss

Wise men always come to the truth
Sooner or later he will figure out you
And when he does – Kiss Kiss

Ascent

Shhhh...I hear something
What is that muffled distant sound?
The faintest tiny voice buried underground

Look carefully I think I see a light
A tiny crack through these deep dark dungeon walls
A single miniscule ray of hope - life's only cure-all

Feel around find the tunnel exiting to faith
Ascend slowly the slippery ragged stairs
Don't be a coward you're the only one who cares

Inhale deeply the clean crisp scent of today
Smell the sweet aroma of hope in the air
Look forward to tomorrow only if you dare

To Be Continued

How did you come to mean so much?
Was it your gentle words or your gentle touch?
I can't imagine my world without you
It's hard to believe that it all came true

You are such an integral part of the puzzle
With twists and turns that seem endless
And a smile that dazzles the world around me
As bright as the stars dancing in the night sky

You came at such an unexpected time
When chaos and sadness seemed to be mine
And gave me a reason to move forward again
We held hands and declared ourselves friends

There is no end to this amazing story
So I have no words to jot down
Forever this thing between me and you
I guess all I can say is, to be continued.........

Demons

My demons are my constant companions
Never wandering far from my thoughts
Safely tucked in the corners of gray matter
Weaving threads like the black widow spider

Their little voices constantly whisper from my ear
Taking full delight in igniting my fire of fear
Turning the heat up to a roaring blaze
Until my world fills with doubts' full haze

My demons have small friends on the outside
Who feed off their poison so they can survive
Venom dripping from their wide, eager mouths
Relishing the sweet taste of fear and doubt

So why do I let these miserable creatures rule?
When their intentions are so clearly sinister and cruel
My demons and their friends are masters at their craft
And often parade through the streets their identities masked

I have learned their tricks and am working without rest
And will tame my demons someday
I have let them run amuck far too long
And will not stop until each one is gone

As for their small friends who feed off of them
For sure they will find another demon friend
They have no power to stand on their own
And will always need to feed from others tired bones

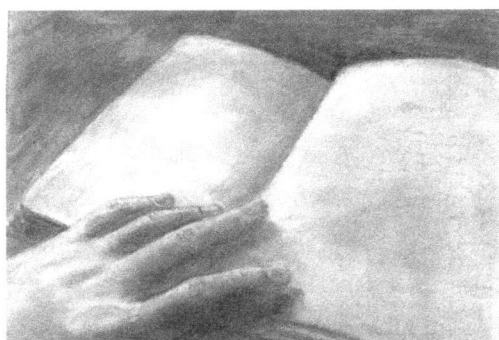

Little Princess

Sweet beautiful princess I miss you so much
How did we end up with this distance between us?
Each day that passes seems like an eternity
We were meant to be together, you and me

I miss your precious smile that you share with such ease
And your happy, happy eyes that always want to please
I miss your huge bear hugs that last endlessly
And our long talks about life and all the insanity

Baby, I want to hear your voice always bursting with news
I want to see you show off those new pair of shoes
Tell me the latest drama starring all the girls and the guys
And play your newest songs, it always make me cry

I love you more than words can express
We need to be together and put my loneliness to rest
Shall I come to you or you come to me?
Makes no difference, as long as it's not merely a dream

Say It

The three most important words in the universe
We all desperately want to hear
The purest most amazing gift
To whisper in someone's sweet ear

Sacred words that should not be said lightly
For they are entwined in honor and trust
When in earnest should be given freely
Three words that define life's quest

We have spent so much time dancing
Not wanting to expose our true thoughts
We use every other expression
But have not dared to spill our hearts

Tomorrow is always a mystery
Never knowing what each moment will bring
I want you to know my true feelings
I want you to know everything

With angst I muster the courage to tell you
For no one should be embarrassed to say
Those three words that mean everything
Baby, I love you in the purest of ways

Believe

I believe in you, all of you
I trust in your beautiful pure heart
And have faith in the pillars of your soul
I accept all of you, just the way you are

We all have blemishes and imperfections
That we do not want the world to see
Parts of our story that we want hidden
Because we think people would flee

There are no chapters in your book
That would cause me to turn from you
I wasn't searching for perfection
The day you appeared in my world

God blessed you with rare and beautiful gifts
To draw the universe to your side
To share your stories with dignity and grace
Infusing those listening with eternal hope and faith

I believe you have been entrusted with the power
To make the world a better place
I have witnessed it already happening
One word, one moment changes everything

I see you at times speckled with doubt
I guess we all have that disease
Sometimes it is difficult to look in the mirror

And see what others so readily can see

My belief in you has no boundaries
And nothing can change its course
I will stand by you and help you believe
In yourself, in your gifts meant for the world to see

Dress Rehearsal

How many times will we practice?
The last scene of our lives
How many times will I mess up my lines?
And break down and cry

You'd think that I would have memorized
The script of our life's play
You would think that I would be ready
For the performance on show day

The characters we play seem so real
I am in love with the lead man
And am quite sure that he loves me too
We're trapped in this plot unable to break through

How many more dress rehearsals?
Before we hit the real stage
Let's never take that last curtain call
Let's embrace love, life's only cure all

Sliding

When did life take that dark turn?
And send you back in time
Your crutches and meds are back in play
Are they temporary or here to stay?

Why does this keep happening?
What triggers such a steep slide?
I watch as you slowly and cautiously ascend
Only to get knocked back down

Your eyes have lost their perfect brilliance
And now are a dull and distant stare
Your smile has become forced and plastic
It seems you are barely here

My heart is aching and shedding tears
That you are back in this sad place
My hands feel so helpless
Not able to hold you in place

I cannot stop this sliding
You are the only one who can do that
But know I will do my very best
To help you on the climb back

www.ingramcontent.com/pod-product-compliance
Lightning Source LLC
LaVergne TN
LVHW092317080426
835509LV00034B/565